Doors to the Sky

First published in 2013 by Grass Roots Press

Grass Roots Press gratefully acknowledges the financial support for its publishing programs provided by the following agencies: the Government of Canada through the Canada Book Fund and the Government of Alberta through the Alberta Foundation for the Arts.

Library and Archives Canada Cataloguing in Publication

Reiff, Tana
    Doors to the sky / Tana Reiff. — Rev. ed.

(Pathfinders)
Previous title: Door is open.
ISBN 978–1–927499–71–9

    1. Readers (Adult). 2. Readers for new literates.
I. Reiff, Tana. Door is open. II. Title. III. Series:
Pathfinders (Edmonton, Alta.)

PE1126.A4R442 2013   428.6'2   C2012–906780–6

Cover image: © Tim Pannell/Corbis

Printed and bound in Canada.

PATHFINDERS

Grass Roots Press

Ducts to the Sky

Tane Keif

Chapter 1

Leena looked up
at the door.
She read the sign:
ADULT SCHOOL
EVERYONE WELCOME!

She was scared to death.
She stood
at the big, heavy door
for a long time.
She peered
through the glass
to see inside.
She put her hand
on the push bar.
Then, at last,
she took a deep breath
and opened the door.

Leena had thought
about this day
for many years.
She had wanted
to finish school
for a long time.
Now she was here.
The time was now.

As she walked
down the hall
she looked back
at the door.
Still time to back out,
she was thinking.

Then she came
to the front desk
of the school.
The woman
behind the desk
was pretty,
with a nice smile.
"Hello!" she said.
"What is your name?"

"My name is Leena,"
said the new student.

"How can we help you?"
the woman asked.

"I want
to finish high school,"
said Leena.

The woman could hear
the way Leena spoke.
She could tell
that Leena's first language
was not English.
"When did you come
to this country?"
she asked.

"I am in this country
since 16 years of age,"
said Leena.
"My family
sent me here
to be married."

"Your English
is very good,"
said the woman.

"Not good enough,"
said Leena.
"I want to read and write
better English.
And I want
a high school diploma."

"Why now?"
the woman asked.

"My children
are teenagers,"
said Leena.
"I gave them
my whole life
for many years.
Now it is my turn.
I want to learn.
I want to get
a good job."

"Ready when you are!"
said the woman
at the desk.

"I am ready!"
said Leena.
"Just one more thing
before I start.
My husband
does not know
I am here.
Please do not tell him."

Chapter 2

Leena thought about
her home country
every day of her life.
In her mind,
she saw the hills
where she grew up.
The air
was so clean.
There were
only blue skies
all around.
Life was hard,
but simple.

Then Leena's uncle
went to look
for a better life
on the other side
of the world.
He wrote back

that he had found
a husband for Leena.
His name was Omar.

The young Leena
did not want to leave
her home.
It was all she knew.
She was only 16.
Omar was 28.

She would always remember
her mother's words.
"Only from the heart
can you touch the sky,"
her mother had said.

To which Leena had said,
with hope in her heart,
"May it be so."

And then her mother said,
"Peace be upon you."

So Leena left her home.
Her uncle met her
at the airport
on the other side
of the world.
He took her
to meet Omar.
Her new life
had begun.

Omar had
his own business.
He sold used cars.
He was doing well.

Leena married Omar.
In the next few years
they had four children.
The family lived
in a big, pretty house.
Leena did not have to work
outside the home.
She had a good life.

But money
did not give Leena
everything she wanted.
Omar was in charge
of her life.
He told her
what to do
and when to do it.
Leena watched
as Omar ran his business.
He showed her
how to keep the books.

She watched her children
learn and grow.
They did well
in school.
They followed their hearts
and reached for the sky.
Leena remembered
her mother's words:
*Only from the heart
can you touch the sky.*
She didn't know

what she herself
was reaching for.
But she too
longed to reach
for the sky.

The doors to the sky
had always been open
for Omar.
Now maybe
the doors can open
for me, too,
Leena thought.

Chapter 3

Adult school
opened Leena's first door.
She loved it.
She couldn't believe
how fast
she was learning.

"You speak English
pretty well,"
Liz, the teacher,
told her.
"That helps you learn
to read and write English.
But how do you know
so much math?"

"I keep the books
for my husband's business,"
Leena said.

"I see,"
said Liz.
"You already know
a lot of what
we're doing in class.
You're just opening
the door of your mind!"

Most of all,
Leena enjoyed
learning *about* English.
She asked Liz
to teach her
about verb tenses.
She learned
that she had been
using simple tenses
too much.
She started using
different verb tenses.

Leena really enjoyed
writing and spelling.
She already knew

most of the words.
She had listened
to people talking.
She had watched TV.
She had helped her children
with their homework.

The English language
was coming together
for Leena.
She became
the best student
in the class.
She felt good.
With every new day,
she felt less scared.
She felt herself moving
just a little closer
to the sky.

Chapter 4

Leena tried
to keep her secret
from Omar.
She went to school
after he left
for the car lot.
She got home each day
before he did.

Then one day
she got home late.
Omar met her
at the door.

"Where have you been?"
he wanted to know.

Leena could not lie
to her husband.
"I go to school,"
she said.

"To school?"
said Omar.
"What for?"
You have
everything you need.
You have plenty to do
right here.
You don't need
to go to school!"

"I want
to finish school,"
said Leena.

"*I* never
finished school,"
Omar said.
"But that didn't stop me
from making money.
Besides, my dear wife,
a woman's place
is in the home."

Leena hated
to hear him say that.

She wanted to say,
"We are not
in the old country.
Times have changed."
But she said nothing.

"I need you
to do my books,"
Omar added.
"And take care
of the house.
And take care
of the kids.
You were born
to do these things."

"You got to choose
your own life,"
said Leena softly.
"You chose
to come here
and sell cars.
I never had
a choice.

Lidia

The choice
was made for me.
I was sent here
and that was that."

"You have a good life!"
said Omar.
He was getting angry.

"My life
is very nice,"
said Leena.
"I thank you for that.
But I want
to finish school.
This is something
I really want to do.
What is wrong
with that?"

This time,
it was Omar
who said nothing.
But he did not look
pleased.

Chapter 5

Leena kept on
going to school.
She wanted to pass
the high school test.
She felt
a long way
from being ready.
She did not
talk to Omar
about school.
She didn't tell him
how much she enjoyed
her English class.
She worked at home
on her math and reading
while he was at work.

Leena was so good
at English
that she helped

other students.
There were students
from many countries.
Leena got along
with everyone.
And everyone
liked Leena.

Once a year,
the adult school
had a big party.
It was time
for this year's party.
Everyone brought
something to eat.
There were foods
from all over the world.

Leena made a dish
from her home country.
Everyone loved it.
Leena was happy
to share her good cooking.

Then some students
started to dance.
Leena had not danced
since she was a young girl.
And she did not know
how to dance
the way the others
were dancing.
But they pulled
on her arm.
Before she knew it,
she was dancing too.

Then Leena said,
"Let me teach you
a dance from my country."
It was an old folk dance.
The others watched
how Leena moved
her arms and hands.
They clapped their hands
along with her.
Before long, everyone
was dancing and clapping.

Leena thought,
What would Omar say
if he saw me now?
Then she tried
not to think about it.
She was having
too much fun.

Chapter 6

The big test
was two weeks away.
Leena was working hard.
But she was
getting scared again.
She wanted
to pass that test
more than anything.
She wasn't sure
that she was ready.

She took
a practice test
on a computer.
"I do believe
you can pass,"
said Liz, the teacher.

"Oh, I hope so,"
said Leena.

"But even if I pass,
Omar won't like it.
He still doesn't think
I should be going
to school."

The night before the test,
Leena wanted to study.
"But I don't know
how much I can do,"
she told Liz.
"Omar will be home tonight."

Liz shook her head.
"Maybe someday
Omar will change."

"You don't know
my Omar!"
Leena said.

That night,
Omar was sitting
in front of the TV.

Behind his back,
Leena took her books
into the bedroom.
She closed
the bedroom door.
She stayed
as quiet as a mouse.

All of a sudden,
the bedroom door
burst open.
"What are you doing?"
yelled Omar.

"I am getting ready
for the big test,"
said Leena.

Omar's veins
were popping
out of his head.
"Why are you
doing this to me?"

"I am not
doing this *to you*,"
said Leena.
"I'm doing this *for me*."

Omar's arms
were flapping.
"I do not see
why you need
to finish school,"
he said.
"Are you trying
to make me look
like a stupid fool?"

"Of course not,"
said Leena.

"I need you
at the car lot
tomorrow morning,"
Omar said.

"I will come
to the car lot,"
said Leena.
"But not until
the test is over."

Omar shook his head.
Then he slammed the door
and went back
to the TV.

Chapter 7

Morning came.
The day of the big test.
Leena woke up
with the sun.
It was early,
but she got up.
She got dressed
and took another look
at the study materials.

"Meet you
at the car lot,"
said the note
she wrote for Omar.

She left the house
without a sound.
She walked
all the way
to the school.

She had to take
that test.
Today.
She knew in her heart
she could pass it.
And she knew in her heart
that she wanted this.
*Only from the heart
can you touch the sky.*
But the rest of her body
was shaking.

She got to the school
an hour early.
She was
the first one there.
The door
was still locked.
She sat on the step
and looked at her books
one last time.

One by one,
the other students
from Leena's class
showed up.
Leena helped them study
at the last minute.
They thought of her
as their second teacher,
after Liz.
Leena made them
feel better
about the test.

At last,
someone came
and opened the door.
Everyone went inside
and took a seat
in front of a computer.
It was time
for the test
to begin.

Omar was gone
from Leena's mind.
She was focused
on the test
and only the test.
In her head,
she went over the tips
Liz had given the class.
Read the whole question.
Answer every question.
Go back to a question
you can't answer right away.
If you don't know the answer,
take a guess.
Keep your eye
on the clock.
Follow all the rules.

And breathe,
Liz had said.
Don't forget to breathe!

Leena took
a deep breath.

Then she began.
Her focus was sharp.
Her breath stayed strong.
She filled in every box.
She worked out
all the math questions.
She typed a response
to each question
needing a longer answer.

She took short breaks
to close her eyes,
rest her mind,
and breathe.
The time went fast.

And then,
she was finished.

She took
the deepest breath of all
and walked outside.
She saw
the bus coming.

She hopped on
and rode to the car lot.

"It's about time
you got here!"
was all Omar said.
His eyes
cut into hers.

Leena knew
her husband.
He was not pleased.

Chapter 8

Test scores
would be online
the next day.
But that one day
did not go fast
for Leena.
She tried
to keep busy.
She finished
all her work
for Omar's business.
She cleaned
the house.
She cooked
a big dinner.
She baked cookies
for her son's team.

She looked online.
No scores posted yet.

She came back
and tried again.
Still no scores.
Then, at last,
the scores showed up.
Right away,
she called Liz.

"I passed!"
she cried.

"I knew you would!"
said Liz.
"I'm so happy for you!
I didn't call you
because I thought
Omar would tell you."

"Omar?"
Leena asked.

"Yes," said Liz.
"He called me
from the car lot
a little while ago

and I told him.
I hope
that was all right!"

"I hope so too,"
said Leena.

Liz went on.
"You had
a very high score.
Have you thought
about going on
with your studies?
You have been so good
at helping
the other students.
You would make
a great teacher."

"I would love
to keep going,"
said Leena.
"But I can't.
It would make Omar
look bad."

Just then,
Leena looked
out the window.
There was Omar.
He was driving
a very nice car
from his lot.

"I must go,"
Leena told Liz.
"Omar just got home.
Liz, I love you!
Thank you so much
for all your help!"

Omar burst in
with a smile
on his face.

"You're home early,"
Leena said to him.
"What's going on?"

"Come outside,"
said Omar.
"Come and see
your new car!"

Leena followed him.
She had seen the car
on the lot.
It was the kind of car
she had always wanted.

"You passed the test!"
said Omar.
"I give each child a car
when they finish school.
You finished school.
So you get a car too.
I hope you like it!"

Chapter 9

After Leena
passed the big test,
she spent more time
at the car lot.

One day
she brought up
the idea
of becoming a teacher.

"Are you talking about
going to university?"
Omar asked.
"That will take years!"

"Yes, I know,"
said Leena.
"I want to do it.
Will you pay for it?"

"Why would you
want to be a teacher?"
Omar went on.
"Why do you want
more school?
Isn't this enough?"

"Do you think I'm trying
to get ahead of you?"
Leena asked.
"I am not!
It's just that
I was good at helping
the other students
at adult school.
Liz told me
I would make
a great teacher.
I think she's right!
I opened one door.
Now I want
to open the next door."

"What about the
children?"
Omar asked.
"What about the house?"

"The children
are not little anymore,"
said Leena.
"The house
doesn't have to be perfect
all the time."

"Yes, it does!"
said Omar.
"And what about
my business?
I still need you
to do my books."

"Don't worry,"
said Leena.
"I'll just have to
plan my time.
I can go to university
part-time at first."

Omar threw his head back
and laughed.
"There is
no stopping you,
is there?"

Leena knew
that was Omar's way
of saying yes.

Chapter 10

A small university
was not far
from Leena's home.
She had seen it,
driving by.
Today she drove
in her new car
to have a look.
The iron gate
was much bigger
than the heavy door
at the adult school.
It scared her
a little bit.
But not like
that first door had.

Leena found the building
she was looking for.
The sign said:

ADMISSIONS.

She sat down
with a middle-aged man.
"So you want to be
a teacher!"
he began.
"What do you
want to teach?"

"I don't know,"
said Leena.
"I loved
studying English.
And I loved helping
the other students."

"You could teach English
to speakers
of other languages,"
said the man.
"Many, many people
want to learn English,
you know."

"But English
is not my first language,"
said Leena.

"So you know
how it feels
to learn English,"
said the man.

Leena remembered
her first few years
in this country.
She had used
her ears and her eyes.
She had picked up
the language
and then got even better
at adult school.

"Yes, I know
how it feels
to learn English,"
Leena said.

"Learning English
is so hard.
Sometimes you feel stupid.
Sometimes you can't find
the right word."

"Knowing how it feels
can help make you
a better teacher."

The man looked
at her test scores
and smiled.
"Yes," he said.
"You could become
a teacher of English.
Would you like
to apply for admission?"

"I would love to,"
said Leena.
"Please tell me
how to start."

Chapter 11

Leena started
by taking some tests
to find out
what she already knew.
She got credit
for three courses
just by passing tests.

Then it was time
to choose courses.
Leena did not want
to get in over her head.
So she chose
just two courses
to start with.

Those first two courses
were not easy.
But Leena did not
let herself be scared.

She did
all the reading.
She listened
to every word
in class.
She asked questions.
She did her homework.
She kept up.

But Leena could see
that time had passed.
She was not as young
as she once was.

For one thing,
there were no books.
All the course materials
were online.
She did her reading
from a screen.

For another thing,
most of the other students
seemed so young.

Leena was old enough
to be their mother.
But she wasn't
the only one.
There were other
older men and women
in her classes.

Then one day
a young student
stopped Leena after class.
His name was Gabe.

"You were so smart
in class today!"
Gabe told Leena.
"Can you help me
go over that material?"

Leena needed to get home.
She didn't really
have time right now.

But Gabe was so cute.
He made Leena think

of her own son.
So she went with him
to the student café.
He bought her
a cup of coffee.
Leena was his teacher
for the next hour.

"Thanks so much!"
Gabe said
as they left the café.
"Can we do this
next week?"

I don't have time
for this,
Leena thought to herself.
But she heard herself saying,
"Sure, we can meet again
next week."

"And may I
bring a few friends?"
Gabe asked.

That week,
Leena went to classes.
She did her homework.
She met with Gabe
and his friends.
She did Omar's books.
(That went a long way
in keeping him happy.)
She cooked meals
ahead of time.
The children helped
around the house.

Leena was moving
like a wind storm.
She did everything
she said she would do.
And then she did more.
She was tired at times.
But she felt good.
The trick
was to keep moving.

And, Leena did
what Liz had told her
before she took the test.
She didn't forget
to breathe.

Chapter 12

The hard work
paid off.
Leena was a star
in the first two courses.

Then it was time
for winter break.
She was so ready
to take some time off.
She caught up
with little jobs
around the house.
She spent time
with her family.
And she could breathe
without telling herself to.

Then it was time to start
two new courses.

"Are you sure
you want to go back?"
Omar asked Leena.

"Of course, I do!"
said Leena.
"I want to finish
what I started.
Besides, Omar,
I like it!"

"Do you really?"
Omar asked.
"Sometimes I think
this whole thing
is killing you.
Wouldn't you rather
take it easy?"

"What for?"
said Leena.
"I want to be
a teacher.
I know it's like

reaching for the sky.
But my heart
is in it.
My mother always said,
'Only from the heart
can you touch the sky.'
So this is what
I need to do
with my life
right now."

Omar knew
that this was true.
He didn't fight about it
like he once did.
He wanted Leena
to be happy.

"Now let me
ask *you* something,"
Leena went on.
"Have *you* ever
thought about going
back to school?"

Omar laughed
his big laugh.
"Me?" he said.
"Why should I
go to school?"

Leena told Omar
about a night course
at the university.
It was called
How to Make More Money
from Your Business.
It was for people
who already had
a business.
It was about ways
to get the word out
and sell more.
The course ran
one evening a week
for six weeks.

"You always want
to make more money,"

said Leena.
"This course
could give you ideas.
Why don't you
sign up?"

"I can't take a course
at the university,"
Omar said.
"I never finished
high school."

"That's okay,"
said Leena.
"These night courses
are open to anyone."

"Then maybe I will go,"
said Omar.
"Maybe I just will.
You don't have to be
the only student
in this house
over the age of 18!"

"Just one thing, Omar,"
Leena added.
"Don't think
I'll give you a car
if you finish
this business course!"

Now Omar was smiling.
"Will you drive me
to school?"
he asked.
"Will you
open the door
for me?"

Leena smiled
at her husband.
"The doors are open,"
she said.
"All you have to do
is walk in.
The first step
is the hardest."

"You are right,
my dear wife,"
said Omar.
"It just took me
a long time
to see that."

"The sky's the limit,"
said Omar's dear wife.
"You just have to
reach for it."

Pathfinders

If you enjoyed this book, you will enjoy these other Pathfinders titles by Tana Reiff.

A Robot Instead
Change Order
Chicken by Charlie
Just for Today
Play Money
Take Away Three
The Saw That Talked
Time to Talk